Melbourne

Travel Guide

2024

An Exclusive Travel Book for Unveiling Melbourne's Enchanting Landscape, Must-see Attractions, Hidden Gems, and Stunning Architecture

Natasiya G. Gwen

TABLE OF CONTENTS

10.3 Local Etiquette and Cultural Tips
10.4 Recommended Itineraries
Conclusion

CHAPTER 1:

Welcome to Melbourne

Welcome, fellow adventurers, to Melbourne, the Southern Hemisphere's doorway to sophistication, where each street corner tells a tale and every laneway whispers secrets about its rich history and lively culture. In the following pages, we will take you on a journey through the heart of Melbourne as we introduce the Melbourne Travel Guide 2024, a unique odyssey into the essence of a city that perfectly blends tradition and modernity.

This is more than just a guide; it's a tailored experience, a key to unlocking the fascinating landscape, discovering hidden jewels, and admiring the breathtaking architecture that marks Melbourne's skyline. As the pages turn, we ask you to look beyond the apparent, to discover not just the must-see sights, but also the throbbing rhythm of the city's many neighborhoods, as well as the eclectic tapestry of its gastronomic, artistic, and sporting offerings.

Melbourne, frequently referred to as Australia's cultural capital, is a city that combines innovation and history. Whether you're a first-time tourist or an experienced explorer, our travel guide will help you navigate this mosaic of treasures. Discover the secret laneways covered with graffiti art, enjoy in the world-renowned coffee culture, see architectural wonders that endure the test of time, and immerse yourself in the kaleidoscope of festivals and events that exuberantly paint the city.

As the sun sets over the Yarra River, Melbourne transforms into a city that never sleeps, alive with the hum of the arts, the cheers of sports fans, and the fragrances of many cuisines. Join us as we explore Melbourne's bustling streets, exploring the stories that make it a unique destination.

Melbourne Travel Guide 2024 is more than simply a guidebook; it's an invitation to be captured, enthralled, and to create memories that will last long after your journey has ended. So strap your seatbelts, turn the pages, and let the adventure begin. Melbourne welcomes you: unique, intriguing, and yours to discover.

1.1 Introduction to Melbourne 2024

Melbourne in 2024 is a city that brings life to every street, laneway, and open space. With its diverse population and palpable energy, Melbourne exemplifies the peaceful coexistence of tradition and modernity. From the famous skyline dominated by architectural marvels to the complex graffiti art concealed in narrow laneways, Melbourne welcomes you to discover its many sides.

The city is a dynamic center for creativity, innovation, and cultural diversity. As you explore its neighborhoods, you'll find a mix of historical significance and contemporary energy. Melbourne has a way of making every visitor feel like they're a part of its unique tapestry, which weaves together stories of indigenous ancestry, European settlement, and a vibrant contemporary culture.

1.2 Brief History and Cultural Overview

To properly appreciate Melbourne, one must explore its rich history. Founded in 1835, the city has grown from a modest colonial outpost to a thriving metropolis. The architecture of heritage-listed buildings has traces of its past, with each conveying a tale of the city's evolution and transformation.

Aboriginal cultures, particularly the Wurundjeri, have had an indelible impact on the city's identity. Respect for indigenous heritage is prevalent across Melbourne's cultural landscape.

As you explore, you'll uncover public artworks, cultural events, and sites that pay honor to the original stewards of the land.

1.3 Practical Information for Travelers

Melbourne's charm goes beyond its captivating past. Practical knowledge is necessary for a smooth exploration of the city. Understanding the public transportation system, currencies, and local customs will improve your overall experience.

Getting Around Melbourne:

The city has an effective public transit system, which includes trains, trams, and buses. The Myki card is your key to hassle-free travel, allowing you to easily navigate Melbourne's huge network. For those who prefer to stroll, the city's grid structure is pedestrian-friendly, and each street offers distinct delights.

Weather and seasons:

Melbourne's weather is often erratic. Locals frequently joke that you can experience four seasons in one day. Summers might be hot, and winters can provide cool mornings. Layered clothing and a lightweight jacket are recommended to ensure you're prepared for any weather.

Currency and tipping:

The Australian dollar (AUD) is the official currency. Tipping is less customary in Australia than in other nations, however it is valued for excellent service. In restaurants, it is common to round up the bill, and a 10% tip is considered generous.

Safety and health:

Melbourne is generally considered a safe place for tourists. Emergency services, including healthcare, are easily accessible. It is recommended that you have travel insurance, and if you have any specific health issues, be aware of the locations of medical clinics and pharmacies.

Language:

Although English is the official language, Melbourne's cultural variety means that a wide range of languages are spoken here. Even if English isn't your first language, the locals are polite and appreciate your efforts to converse.

Local Etiquettes:

Australians are known for their easygoing and welcoming disposition. When in Melbourne, a casual and respectful manner is preferred. Queuing is a cultural norm, and saying "please" and "thank you" can go a long way in conversations.

As you prepare to immerse yourself in Melbourne's colorful landscape, armed with historical insights and practical information, you're ready to embark on an adventure full of discoveries. Melbourne awaits, eager to reveal its secrets and create an unforgettable impression on your trip memories.

CHAPTER 2:

Navigating Melbourne's Neighborhoods

Melbourne, the dynamic hub of Victoria, is distinguished by its different and distinctive neighborhoods, each with its own personality and charm. In this chapter, we will go across the different landscapes of Melbourne's neighborhoods, unraveling the tapestry that makes this city a captivating destination for all visitors.

2.1 Exploring the Central Business District (CBD)

The Central Business District (CB) is the beating heart of Melbourne, a dynamic metropolis where modernity and tradition coexist. Skyscrapers embellished with elegant glass facades coexist with old buildings, resulting in a unique skyline. Wander along Collins Street, often known as the "Paris End," to find high-end shopping, expensive eating, and hidden laneways lined with boutique shops and cafes.

Federation Square is a cultural center and meeting place for both locals and visitors in the CBD. It's a must-see monument that hosts events and festivals while also exhibiting architectural marvels. Take a stroll down the Yarra River, where the bustling Southbank region boasts riverside promenades, entertainment complexes, and breathtaking vistas of the city.

2.2 Southbank: Riverside Elegance

Crossing the Yarra River from the CBD, Southbank reveals a world of sophistication and elegance. Riverside eating, cultural organizations such as the Arts Centre Melbourne, and the Crown Entertainment Complex distinguish this neighborhood. Enjoy a riverfront supper with breathtaking views of the city lights, or see a show at one of Southbank's renowned theaters.

For visitors looking to unwind, the Southbank Promenade offers a leisurely stroll along the river, complete with public art works and attractive cafes. As the sun sets, the city lights illuminate the water, creating a magnificent atmosphere that encapsulates the essence of Southbank.

2.3 Fitzroy: Bohemian Vibes and Street Art

Travel north to Fitzroy, Melbourne's bohemian quarter, where street art, quirky stores, and eclectic eateries create a vibrant picture of creativity. Explore the historic Brunswick Street, which is known for its alternative fashion, vintage shops, and bustling ambiance. Fitzroy is a paradise for art aficionados, with graffiti-covered laneways that showcase the city's thriving street art scene.

In addition to its artistic flair, Fitzroy features a diversified gastronomic scene. From trendy brunch spots to secret pubs, this area encourages you to experience the distinct flavors that distinguish Melbourne's culinary environment.

2.4 St Kilda: Beachside Bliss

A short tram journey from the city center will transport you to St Kilda, where the city meets the sea. This classic coastal area is famous for its vibrant atmosphere, Luna Park's historic amusement rides, and the landmark St Kilda Pier. Take a leisurely stroll along the Esplanade, discover Acland Street's unique cafes and cake stores, and unwind on St Kilda Beach with the Melbourne skyline as a backdrop.

St Kilda also has a vibrant nightlife scene. From seaside pubs to live music venues, St Kilda's evenings are just as vibrant as the days. Don't miss the spectacular sunset across Port Phillip Bay from the end of St Kilda Pier.

2.5 Carlton: Academic Charm and Gardens

Carlton, located just north of the CBD, is Melbourne's intellectual and cultural core. This suburb, which is home to the University of Melbourne, radiates intellectual charm with its leafy lanes, historic architecture, and eclectic mix of academic and creative enterprises.

Immerse yourself in the peacefulness of the Royal Exhibition Building and Carlton Gardens, both of which are UNESCO World Heritage sites. The Melbourne Museum, located within the complex, houses a wealth of natural and cultural heritage. Carlton is also known for its Italian background, which is evident in the abundance of real trattorias and espresso cafes that line the streets.

In this chapter, we've only touched the surface of Melbourne's many neighborhoods. Each one tells a distinct tale, enabling you to discover Melbourne's varied personality and the hidden gems that make it such an attractive place.

CHAPTER 3:
A Culinary Journey Through Melbourne

Melbourne, often regarded as Australia's food capital, has a culinary scene as broad and eclectic as the city itself. In this chapter, we take a gastronomic journey through Melbourne's streets, discovering the city's rich tapestry of flavors, scents, and culinary traditions that make it a foodie's paradise.

3.1 Melbourne's Diverse Food Scene

Melbourne's cuisine culture reflects its multicultural population. From Italian trattorias to Asian hawker stalls, the city's culinary scene is a fusion of worldwide influences. Begin your adventure by meandering through the Central Business District's (CBD) laneways, where hidden jewels and hole-in-the-wall cafes serve a diverse range of international food. Within a few blocks, you may have authentic Greek souvlaki, Vietnamese pho, and traditional Italian pizza.

Exit the CBD and explore neighborhoods such as Fitzroy and Brunswick, which are famed for their hipster cafes and fusion restaurants. These areas encourage experimentation, blending traditional recipes with new tweaks to create foods that surprise and thrill the taste buds.

3.2 Iconic Cafés and Coffee Culture

No visit to Melbourne's culinary scene is complete without experiencing the city's famed coffee culture. Melbourne takes coffee seriously, with a vibrant cafe culture that has catapulted the city to the status of a global coffee destination. Cafés in Melbourne are more than simply locations to get your caffeine fix; they are centers of creativity, community, and conversation.

Explore the alleyways and hidden corners to find cafes where baristas lovingly prepare each cup. Melbourne's coffee scene has something for everyone, whether you want a standard flat white or want to try something new. Don't be shocked if you find yourself discussing the ideal bean roast or the subtleties of pour-over brewing with local coffee enthusiasts.

3.3 Food Markets and Street Eats

To properly understand Melbourne's food culture, immerse yourself in the colorful ambiance of its food markets. Queen Victoria Market, a historic site, provides a sensory overload with stalls selling fresh fruit, artisanal cheeses, and international cuisines. Explore the multicultural part of the market to find spices, herbs, and foods from all over the world, making it a culinary heaven for home cooks and food lovers.

For a more relaxed dining experience, try street food. Melbourne's food trucks and pop-up booths demonstrate the city's dedication to diversified, on-the-go cuisine. Wander the streets during culinary festivals or night markets, where you can sample anything from gourmet burgers and loaded fries to exotic desserts. It's a visual and culinary delight.

3.4 Fine Dining Gems

While Melbourne values casual and street-side dining, it also has a sophisticated side with a number of world-class fine dining restaurants. Explore restaurants that transform dining into a holistic experience and immerse yourself in the world of culinary art. Melbourne's fine dining scene offers degustation meals using locally sourced ingredients as well as avant-garde concoctions that push the boundaries of flavor.

Consider legendary venues such as Attica, which is frequently listed among the world's greatest restaurants, and where Chef Ben Shewry creates meals inspired by Australia's various landscapes. Alternatively, immerse yourself in the riverfront elegance of Vue de Monde, which offers panoramic views of the city and a menu celebrating contemporary Australian cuisine.

In conclusion, Chapter 3 of "Melbourne Travel Guide 2024" encourages readers to experience the rich and dynamic flavors that distinguish Melbourne's culinary landscape. Whether you're a coffee aficionado, a street food fanatic, or someone who enjoys fine dining, Melbourne's culinary scene offers a gourmet trip that embodies the city's cosmopolitan ethos and persistent passion for good cuisine. Prepare for an extraordinary gastronomic excursion that will make an indelible impression on your senses.

CHAPTER 4:

Architectural Marvels of Melbourne

Melbourne, a city that perfectly combines history and modernity, is a treasure mine of architectural marvels. Chapter 4 of the Melbourne Travel Guide 2024 encourages you to explore the city's spectacular architectural landscape. From iconic structures to heritage treasures, Melbourne's architecture reflects its rich history and forward-thinking current.

4.1 Melbourne's Unique Architectural Landscape

Melbourne's architectural diversity reflects the city's evolution. As you walk through its streets, you'll notice a stunning mix of Victorian,

Edwardian, and contemporary styles. Skyscrapers stand cheek to shoulder with historic buildings, forming a visual tapestry that captivates all visitors.

Architects from throughout the world have made their mark on Melbourne, creating a cityscape that is both recognizable and refreshingly new. The contrast between old and modern is underlined at Docklands, where elegant glass towers emerge alongside refurbished warehouses, demonstrating the city's commitment to merging the past and the future.

4.2 Flinders Street Station: A Timeless Icon

No journey of Melbourne's architecture is complete without a stop at Flinders Street Station, the city's iconic landmark. For years, postcards have featured the station's famous yellow exterior and distinctive dome. As you enter the crowded platforms, you'll be surrounded by a diverse range of architectural styles, from the Romanesque entry to the more recent modern additions.

Take a moment to enjoy the complex aspects of the station's construction, from the arched windows to the clocks that have been directing Melbourne residents for over 100 years. Flinders

Street Station is more than just a transit hub; it exemplifies Melbourne's architectural resiliency.

4.3 Eureka Tower: Sky-high Spectacle

For a physical ascension into Melbourne's architectural prowess, head to the Eureka Tower. This soaring skyscraper, standing at 297 meters, is one of the tallest residential buildings in the Southern Hemisphere. The Eureka Tower not only provides panoramic views of the city, but it also exemplifies contemporary design.

Daredevils can visit 'The Edge,' a glass cube that protrudes from the building's 88th story, offering an exciting view of the bustling streets below. The Eureka Tower represents Melbourne's ambition, striving for the sky while remaining firmly rooted in the city's cultural diversity.

4.4 Royal Exhibition Building: Heritage Grandeur

The Royal Exhibition Building, a UNESCO World Heritage site, is a great showcase of Melbourne's nineteenth-century architectural beauty. This masterpiece, located in the Carlton Gardens, was created for the Melbourne International Exhibition in 1880. The building's complex dome and classical design make it a compelling symbol of the city's dedication to conserving its ancient heritage.

Step inside to admire the Great Hall's vast area, which is graced with a spectacular dome that floods the interior with natural light. The Royal Exhibition Building serves as a reminder of Melbourne's growth as a cultural and commercial capital during the Victorian era, inviting visitors to immerse themselves in the grandeur of bygone times.

Explore Melbourne's Architectural Neighborhoods

Beyond these individual marvels, Melbourne's neighborhoods are full of architectural beauties. Wander through the laneways of the Central Business District (CBD) to find a mix of modern skyscrapers and hidden gems buried away in alleys. Southbank, with its riverbank splendor, features a mix of contemporary architecture and waterfront constructions.

Fitzroy, noted for its bohemian character, is filled with Victorian-era buildings converted into fashionable boutiques and cafes. Fitzroy's preservation of old structures exemplifies Melbourne's commitment to honoring its roots while moving forward. St Kilda, with its Art Deco influences, provides insight into the city's architectural history down the coast.

Melbourne Architectural Events and Exhibitions

To completely immerse yourself in Melbourne's architectural environment, plan your visit around events like Melbourne Design Week or Open House Melbourne. These events grant access to previously inaccessible areas, giving attendees an insider's perspective on architectural marvels and the creative minds defining the metropolis.

Architectural walking tours are also popular, as they allow you to learn more about specific neighborhoods and themes. Whether you're interested in heritage preservation, sustainable design, or cutting-edge contemporary architecture, Melbourne has an experience for you.

The Future Of Melbourne's Skyline

Melbourne's skyline is changing as the city evolves. Several major initiatives are underway, promising to transform the cityscape in novel ways. From sustainable skyscrapers to adaptive reuse projects, the future of Melbourne architecture is full of intriguing possibilities.

One such initiative is the Melbourne Arts Precinct Redevelopment, which aims to convert the Southbank region into a world-class cultural destination. With new architectural features, this precinct will reshape Melbourne's cultural environment, demonstrating the city's commitment to encouraging creativity and innovation.

This chapter allows you to admire the architectural symphony that defines this lively city. Melbourne's architectural panorama, from the timeless elegance of Flinders Street Station to the contemporary heights of the Eureka Tower and the historic charm of the Royal Exhibition Building, exemplifies the city's capacity to embrace both the past and the future. As you explore these wonders, you'll realize that Melbourne's architecture is more than simply buildings; it's about the tales they tell and the dynamic energy of a city that is always reinventing itself.

CHAPTER 5:

Unveiling Hidden Gems

Melbourne is more than just a metropolis; it is a treasure trove waiting to be discovered. Beyond the well-known sights and bustling streets lies a secret world of hidden gems just waiting to be discovered by those with a keen eye. Chapter 5 of our special travel book, "Unveiling Hidden Gems," invites you to venture off the main road and discover Melbourne's lesser-known wonders.

5.1 Secret Laneways and Graffiti Art

Melbourne is well-known for its robust street art movement, which takes place on the city's hidden laneways. Walking through these tight corridors is like entering an open-air gallery, with vibrant murals and thought-provoking graffiti covering every corner and hole. One of the most well-known is Hosier Lane, which is a kaleidoscope of creativity, with constantly changing artworks that represent the city's dynamic energy.

As you explore these hidden laneways, keep an eye out for Degraves Street, which is dotted with unique cafes, boutiques, and stunning street art. Each turn provides a fresh surprise, making it an excellent choice for anyone looking for an authentic Melbourne experience away from the masses.

5.2 Hidden Bars and Speakeasies

Melbourne's nightlife is not restricted to conventional venues; the city also has a profusion of underground clubs and speakeasies. These covert venues, hidden behind modest façade, radiate intrigue and exclusivity. One such gem is Eau de Vie, which is hidden behind an unmarked entrance on Malthouse Lane. Inside, you'll find a softly lit, intimate environment with beautifully made drinks and rare spirits.

If you enjoy secret entrances, head to Berlin Bar, where you must pass via a hidden door disguised as a bookshelf. The venue is divided between

East and West Berlin-themed sections, each with its own distinct vibe. Melbourne's hidden bars provide not just outstanding drinks, but also a sense of adventure and discovery for those who seek them out.

5.3 Quirky Museums and Unusual Attractions

Beyond standard museums, Melbourne has a plethora of unusual and wacky institutions that highlight the city's uniqueness. The Old Melbourne Gaol, a former prison, is now a museum that provides terrifying insights into the city's criminal history. Dark cells, creepy gallows, and intriguing exhibits make it a must-see for those who enjoy the macabre.

For something altogether different, visit the Hellenic Museum, housed in the old Royal Mint building. This cultural gem honors the rich tradition of Greek immigrants in Australia with a unique collection of antiquities and contemporary art. It reflects Melbourne's multicultural identity and the various stories that have shaped the city.

If you're looking for something out of the ordinary, visit the Museum of Chinese-Australian History, which is located on Cohen Place. This hidden gem examines the Chinese community's contributions to Melbourne's growth, providing a unique viewpoint on the city's mixed tapestry.

In this chapter, we've only scratched the surface of Melbourne's hidden gems, but the city has much more to offer for those prepared to look beyond the apparent. From hidden laneways covered with street art to secret pubs offering superb cocktails and eccentric museums digging into Melbourne's unique past, this chapter serves as a doorway to the city's hidden gems. As you embark on your adventure of discovery, keep in mind that Melbourne's genuine enchantment is found not just in its well-known attractions, but also in the hidden gems that reveal the heart and soul of this wonderful city.

CHAPTER 6:

Natural Wonders in and Around Melbourne

Melbourne, frequently praised for its urban energy and cultural brilliance, conceals a plethora of natural treasures that enchant both locals and visitors. Chapter 6 of the Melbourne Travel Guide 2024 explores into the magical world of Melbourne's natural environments, taking you through lush green sanctuaries, spectacular coastline vistas, and calm getaways that provide a break from the city's vibrant vitality.

6.1 Royal Botanic Gardens: A Green Oasis

The Royal Botanic Gardens, located in the heart of Melbourne, are a tranquil retreat. These expertly manicured gardens, covering 94 acres, are more than just a collection of plants; they are a living tapestry of botanical diversity. Visitors can meander through themed gardens, each with its own tale, from the timeless grandeur of the Rose Garden to the indigenous flora shown in the Australian Forest Walk. Guilfoyle's Volcano, an extinct volcano turned water reservoir, offers an elevated vantage point with sweeping views of the gardens below.

The Royal Botanic Gardens are more than just a natural escape; they also serve as a cultural hub, offering events, workshops, and exhibitions. The Aboriginal Heritage Walk teaches visitors about the land's rich Indigenous history, and the Moonlight Cinema converts the gardens into an open-air theater throughout the summer months. It's a site where nature and culture coexist, resulting in an experience that goes beyond the ordinary botanical garden visit.

6.2 Great Ocean Road: Coastal Majesty

Take a gorgeous drive down one of the world's most iconic coastal routes, the Great Ocean Road. This meandering road, which hugs the Victorian coastline for 240 kilometers, reveals a sequence of natural treasures that leave an unforgettable imprint on people who travel along it. The Twelve Apostles, a group of limestone stacks rising magnificently from the Southern Ocean, serve as sentinels along this rocky coastline, providing a breathtaking spectacle, particularly at sunrise and sunset.

As you continue your tour, explore Loch Ard Gorge, named after the shipwrecked clipper "Loch Ard." Other geological wonders carved by wind and water are the Arch, London Bridge, and the Grotto. The Great Ocean Road is more than simply a road trip; it's an immersive experience with nature's raw beauty, with possibilities for wildlife viewing, coastal treks, and peaceful contemplation by the ocean's edge.

6.3 Dandenong Ranges: Tranquil Escapes

The Dandenong Ranges, located just a short drive from Melbourne, offer a peaceful getaway into the embrace of nature. This attractive location is characterized by verdant forests, charming villages, and refreshing mountain air. One of the highlights is the Puffing Billy Railway, a century-old steam train that travels through lush fern gullies and towering eucalyptus trees. The renowned William Ricketts Sanctuary, hidden in the Dandenong Ranges, is a sculpture park where art and nature coexist, with clay works seamlessly incorporated into the natural environment.

Explore the Dandenong Ranges National Park's numerous walking routes, which lead to panoramic views, secret waterfalls, and encounters with natural species. The Alfred Nicholas Gardens, with its tranquil lakes and brilliant blossoms, provide a pleasant respite, while the SkyHigh Mount Dandenong Observatory provides a lofty vantage point for panoramic views of Melbourne and beyond.

Time seems to slow down in the Dandenong Ranges, allowing tourists to reconnect with nature in an environment that feels worlds away from the hustle and bustle of the metropolis. From the soothing whisper of a mountain air to the melodic birdsong booming through the treetops, this location provides an immersive experience for those seeking comfort in the arms of the Australian environment.

This chapter invites you to discover the natural beauties that surround the city. Whether you seek peace in the perfectly groomed landscapes of the Royal Botanic Gardens, embark on a coastal expedition along the Great Ocean Road, or seek tranquility in the Dandenong Ranges, Melbourne's natural beauty encourages you to explore a new side of this wonderful city.

CHAPTER 7:

Melbourne's Arts and Culture Scene

Melbourne is not just a city of breathtaking scenery and culinary pleasures, but it is also a bustling center of arts and culture. In Chapter 7 of "Melbourne Travel Guide 2024," we explore Melbourne's rich tapestry of artistic offerings, including famous institutions, immersive experiences, and the city's vibrant cultural life.

7.1 National Gallery of Victoria (NGV)

The National Gallery of Victoria (NGV) is in the vanguard of Melbourne's art scene, perfectly combining classical beauty and contemporary flair. Established in 1861, the NGV has grown into an artistic powerhouse with a vast collection spanning eras and continents.

Visitors to the NGV will be surrounded by a variety of artistic expressions. The gallery's worldwide collection includes European masterpieces, Asian art, and Aboriginal Australian items. Prepare to be enthralled by classic works like Sidney Nolan's "Ned Kelly" series and vivid Indigenous Australian art that portrays the country's old cultural heritage.

One of the NGV's most notable features is its emphasis on modern art. The gallery hosts cutting-edge exhibitions that test the limits of artistic innovation. From immersive installations to thought-provoking performances, the NGV makes every visit a memorable and stimulating experience.

7.2 Melbourne Museum: Tales of the City

The Melbourne Museum, located in Carlton Gardens, is a treasure trove of knowledge as well as a celebration of the city's rich past. Visitors to this architectural masterpiece take a journey through time, viewing displays that depict Melbourne's progression from a colonial outpost to a modern metropolis.

The museum's displays have been painstakingly arranged to provide a thorough overview of Melbourne's cultural, social, and environmental aspects. Wander through the Forest Gallery, a natural rainforest setting that showcases Australia's distinct ecosystems. Explore the

Melbourne Story exhibition, an immersive experience that tells the city's story through relics, multimedia displays, and interactive installations.

For anyone interested in science and technology, the Science and Life Gallery is a must-see. Marvel at nature's wonders and human innovation. From dinosaur fossils to space exploration, the Melbourne Museum welcomes visitors of all ages.

7.3 Performing Arts and Theater District

Melbourne's passion for the performing arts is obvious in its thriving theater sector, where innovation takes center stage. The city is home to various theaters, each with its own distinct personality and charm.

The Arts Centre Melbourne, an architectural wonder located on the banks of the Yarra River, is a popular destination for performing arts fans. The complex includes several venues, including the renowned Arts Centre, Hamer Hall, and the Sidney Myer Music Bowl. The Arts Centre Melbourne provides a varied range of cultural activities, including classical performances by the Melbourne Symphony Orchestra, contemporary plays, and dance productions.

Enter the ancient Princess Theatre, a location that emanates old-world elegance. The Princess Theatre, known for staging blockbuster musicals and dramatic events, encourages visitors to experience the wonder of live performance.

For a taste of the avant-garde, visit Melbourne's independent theater scene, which includes venues such as the Malthouse Theatre and La Mama Theatre. These tiny locations highlight experimental works and nurture young talent, adding to the city's reputation as a breeding ground for artistic creativity.

As night falls, the theater area comes alive with the glow of marquees and the promise of thrilling performances. Whether you're a regular theatergoer or a first-time visitor, Melbourne's performing arts scene is sure to leave an indelible impression on your cultural trip.

In this chapter, we have just scratched the surface of Melbourne's arts and culture sector. From world-class galleries to engaging museums and lively theaters, the city invites visitors to immerse themselves in a tapestry of creation. As you explore Melbourne's cultural treasures, you'll notice that the city's fascination extends beyond its physical beauty, encompassing the artistic spirit that pervades its streets and venues.

CHAPTER 8:

Sporting Capital: Melbourne's Love for Sports

Melbourne, frequently referred to as the "Sporting Capital of the World," pulsates with a passion for sports that is profoundly embedded in its cultural DNA. Chapter 8 of the Melbourne Travel Guide 2024 digs into the heart of this passion, examining landmark venues, important sporting events, and the electrifying atmosphere that distinguishes Melbourne as a global sports destination.

8.1 Melbourne Cricket Ground (MCG)

The Melbourne Cricket Ground (MCG) is at the heart of Melbourne's sports culture, an arena that goes beyond sport to represent community, tradition, and unabashed excitement. This massive stadium, affectionately known as the "G," is not only the world's largest cricket ground, but it is also an iconic location for Australian Rules Football (AFL) and other significant events.

The chapter delves deeply into the history of the MCG, tracing its origins back to 1853 and discussing the occasions that have cemented its place in athletic history. From the roar of the crowd during a great Ashes series to the deafening acclaim of Aussie Rules fans, the MCG exemplifies Melbourne's sporting enthusiasm.

8.2 Australian Open: Grand Slam Excitement

Melbourne comes alive every year with the thrilling Australian Open, one of the four Grand Slam tennis events. The chapter takes readers on a journey through Melbourne Park's courts, where the world's top tennis players compete for supremacy against the backdrop of Melbourne's skyline.

The Australian Open is more than just a tennis tournament; it's a showcase for athleticism, style, and international fellowship. The book provides insights into the best ways to experience the tournament, from acquiring tickets to taking in the vibrant atmosphere in Garden Square.

8.3 Sporting Events and Fan Experiences

Beyond the MCG and the Australian Open, Melbourne's calendar is packed with a broad selection of sporting events, and Chapter 8 delves into the rich tapestry of possibilities accessible to sports fans.

From the scream of engines at the Melbourne Grand Prix to the thunderous hooves at the Melbourne Cup Carnival, this guide covers all of the city's main sporting events. Whether it's the athleticism of the Melbourne Marathon or the sheer spectacle of Supercars racing through the streets, Melbourne has a sports experience for everyone.

The chapter goes beyond the events themselves, delving into the unique fan experiences that make attending these events so memorable. From pre-game rituals to post-game celebrations, Melbourne's sports culture goes far beyond the pitch.

8.4 Sporting Culture: More Than Just Games

Melbourne's love of sports extends beyond the stadiums and pervades the entire city. The book visits the city's sports pubs, where fans meet to cheer on their favorite teams and share in the game's victories and heartbreaks. It goes into local sports talk radio, where impassioned commentators analyze the current sporting dramas.

Furthermore, Melbourne's public spaces, parks, and recreational areas exude a sporting spirit. The guide advises readers to join locals for a game of pickup basketball, try their hand at Australian Rules Football in the park, or even play a friendly game of cricket on a beautiful afternoon.

8.5 Melbourne's Sports Museums and Hall of Fame

The chapter delves on Melbourne's sporting legacy, including its museums and Hall of Fame. From the Australian Tennis Hall of Fame to the Australian Racing Museum, these institutions honor the legends who have defined Melbourne's sporting history.

Visitors may immerse themselves in Australia's rich sporting history, learning about historic moments, renowned sportsmen, and the evolution of sport in Melbourne. The book describes the exhibitions, interactive displays, and special events hosted by these museums, providing a comprehensive experience for sports history aficionados.

This chapter is a riveting excursion into the heart of Melbourne's sports culture. Whether you're a die-hard fan or a casual observer, the chapter seeks to capture the adrenaline, passion, and communal spirit that make Melbourne a true sporting hotspot.

CHAPTER 9:

Festivals and Events in Melbourne

Melbourne, often referred to as Australia's cultural capital, is well-known not only for its gorgeous landscapes and architectural marvels, but also for its vibrant and diversified festival calendar. Chapter 9 of the "Melbourne Travel Guide 2024" welcomes you to discover the city's pulsating heartbeat, where each month brings a new event, whether artistic, culinary, or sporting.

9.1 Melbourne International Comedy Festival

Every year, laughter rings through the streets of Melbourne as the city hosts one of the world's largest and most prestigious comedy festivals.

The Melbourne International Comedy Festival, which takes place in March and April, turns the city into a platform for a variety of hilarious performances. Local performers, international stand-up stars, and budding comedians all come together to tickle the audience's funny bones, making it a must-see event for anybody looking for a dose of humor and entertainment.

The festival covers more than just classic stand-up; it also includes improv, sketch comedy, and experimental performances. Venues throughout the city, from iconic theaters to intimate comedy clubs, present a wide spectrum of comic styles. The festival's inclusive character ensures that there is something for everyone, from family-friendly performances to late-night adult comedy. Whether you're a comedy fan or simply seeking for a good laugh, the Melbourne

International Comedy Festival offers a unique experience.

9.2 White Night Melbourne: A Night of Lights

During the White Night Melbourne festival, Melbourne is transformed into a stunning canvas of lights, colors, and artistic expression as the sun goes down. This annual winter festival transforms the city into an open-air gallery, illuminating famous buildings and public places with magnificent light installations, projections, and interactive artworks. The mood is electrifying as locals and visitors alike walk through the changed streets, admiring the city's attractions bathed in a rainbow of colors.

White Night is more than just a visual feast; it celebrates Melbourne's creative spirit. The festival offers a wide variety of performances, including live music, dance, and immersive art experiences. Venues such as the National Gallery of Victoria (NGV) and Federation Square become foci of activity, hosting both large-scale events and intimate performances. The event's nocturnal nature adds a touch of magic, providing a distinct and magical ambiance that captivates spectators.

9.3 Melbourne Food and Wine Festival

For foodies, the Melbourne Food and Wine Festival is a gastronomic trip through the city's rich and diverse food scene. This event, held every March, brings together elite chefs, winemakers, and food lovers from all over the world for a flavor-filled celebration. The event's broad program includes food and wine tastings, workshops, cooking demos, and unique dining experiences that highlight Melbourne's lively culinary scene.

One of the festival's highlights is the World's Longest Lunch, in which a single, magnificent table spans a prominent metropolitan area, creating a communal dining experience that represents Melbourne's sense of cooperation. From artisanal markets to high-end restaurants, the Melbourne Food and Wine Festival encourages visitors to taste the city's gastronomic delights while promoting a feeling of community and appreciation for delicious food and wine.

Experience Melbourne's Festival Culture

Chapter 9 urges visitors to coincide their visit with one of Melbourne's bustling festivals for a remarkable and engaging experience. Whether you enjoy laughter, the beauty of light and art, or culinary delights, Melbourne's festival scene has something for you. As you navigate the bustling streets and vibrant activities, you'll realize that Melbourne's festivals not only entertain but also offer a unique glimpse into the city's character, where creativity, variety, and a love of life collide. Prepare to be delighted by the city's festive mood, making your visit a fascinating experience of Melbourne's cultural wealth in 2024.

CHAPTER 10:

Practical Tips and Local Insights

Welcome to the final chapter of the Melbourne Travel Guide 2024, where we'll go over the crucial practical recommendations and local insights that will enhance your Melbourne experience. As you embark on this enchanting tour through the city's scenery, attractions, hidden gems, and stunning architecture, arm yourself with these vital details to guarantee a smooth and immersive experience.

10.1 Transportation and Getting Around

Melbourne's transit system is well-connected and efficient, allowing you to easily travel the city. The famous trams are an important part of Melbourne's identity, offering a unique method to get around the city while taking in the sights. Consider obtaining a Myki card to have easy access to trams, buses, and trains.

Cycling around Melbourne is a popular way to get a more customized experience. The city has bike lanes, and several rental programs provide an easy way to pedal through the attractive neighborhoods and scenic trails.

Taxis and ridesharing services are widely available, providing a comfortable and quick form of transportation, particularly for late-night excursions. Furthermore, Melbourne's walkability is a traveler's dream, so don't be afraid to wander through the city's various neighborhoods, discovering hidden gems along the way.

10.2 Accommodation Options

Melbourne has a diverse choice of housing alternatives to suit a variety of interests and budgets. From opulent hotels in the heart of the city to tiny boutique guesthouses in the suburbs, you'll find the ideal location to relax and recharge after a day of adventure.

Consider staying in distinctive accommodations that represent Melbourne's colorful personality, such as converted warehouses, artsy boutique hotels, or eco-friendly lodgings. Accept the local welcome and immerse yourself in the unique charm that each area has to offer.

To fully appreciate Melbourne's uniqueness, consider changing your accommodations between different regions, allowing you to explore the city's varied sides and discover hidden gems that may not be obvious in the bustling city center.

10.3 Local Etiquette and Cultural Tips

Melburnians are noted for their amiable and laid-back nature. Embrace the local culture by striking up casual conversations with locals, who are typically eager to share their favorite places and recommendations.

Tipping is appreciated in restaurants and cafes but is not required. A 10% tip is traditional, but many establishments include a service charge on the bill. Remember that tipping is a show of appreciation for excellent service.

Melbourne values diversity and inclusion. Respectful behavior toward all individuals, regardless of background, is strongly encouraged. Embrace the multicultural atmosphere by sampling cuisine from various ethnic groups and attending cultural events during your stay.

10.4 Recommended Itineraries for Various Interests

To make the most of your stay in Melbourne, plan your itinerary around your interests.

Whether you enjoy food, art, nature, or sports, Melbourne has something for everyone.

For Food Enthusiasts:

Begin the day with a delicious breakfast at a neighborhood café in Fitzroy. Explore Queen Victoria Market for a variety of fresh food and local delights. Spend your evening in Richmond, which is recognized for its numerous eating options, including international food and local favorites.

To Art Lovers:

Immerse yourself in the cultural district by visiting the NGV and discovering the vivid street art on Hosier Lane. Visit the Melbourne Museum for a better knowledge of the city's history and creative influences. In the evening, take in a performance at one of the city's famed theaters.

For nature seekers:

Begin the day with a calm stroll in the Royal Botanic Gardens. Visit the Dandenong Ranges for a picturesque getaway, exploring the lush forests and quaint communities. Finish the day with a sunset walk along St Kilda Beach.

For sports fans:

Take a tour of the Melbourne Cricket Ground (MCG) and learn about the city's sporting heritage. Catch a game or attend a sporting event at one of the city's most famous stadiums. Finish your day with a visit to the Australian Sports Museum, which offers an immersive sports experience.

Melbourne is a city with limitless opportunities and discoveries. By incorporating these practical ideas and local insights into your vacation, you will not only be able to confidently traverse Melbourne but also discover the hidden jewels and unique experiences that make this city so beautiful.

Conclusion

As we complete this special travel guide to Melbourne in 2024, we are filled with awe and appreciation for this intriguing Australian metropolis. Melbourne, a city that perfectly blends tradition and contemporary, has captured the hearts of both residents and visitors.

Our voyage around Melbourne's stunning terrain revealed a city with layers of history, culture, and innovation. From the iconic skyline to the hidden laneways decorated with graffiti art, every corner holds a tale waiting to be told.

Melbourne's culinary scene is broad and wonderful, reflecting the city's cosmopolitan essence. Melbourne welcomes you to appreciate the flavors of its melting pot, whether you're sipping a properly prepared coffee in a cozy laneway café or dining at a great restaurant.

The architectural marvels that dot the metropolitan skyline, from historic sites to modern skyscrapers, demonstrate Melbourne's dedication to maintaining its legacy while still looking forward.

Exploring Melbourne's hidden gems has given you the joy of discovering secret bars, tucked-away museums, and the charm of offbeat neighborhoods, each adding a unique brushstroke to the city's lively canvas.

The natural delights around Melbourne, from the lush greenery of the Royal Botanic Gardens to the spectacular views along the Great Ocean Road, highlight Australia's diverse diversity.

You've observed Melbourne's passion for innovation, competitiveness, and celebration by immersing yourself in the city's vibrant festivals, exploring the arts and cultural scene, and attending sporting events at the historic Melbourne Cricket Ground.

As you prepare to leave this lovely city, keep in mind that Melbourne is more than simply a place to visit; it is an experience. Whether you were looking for adventure, relaxation, gastronomic delights, or cultural immersion, Melbourne met and exceeded your expectations.

May your recollections of Melbourne be filled with laneway laughter, culinary delights, architectural wonders, and warm people. Until we meet again in this metropolitan haven, Melbourne welcomes you back with wide arms, eager to share new stories and reveal more of its ageless allure. Safe travels, and may your link with Melbourne serve as a treasured chapter in your travel journey.

Printed in Great Britain
by Amazon

39471601R00050